VINTAGE WHINES

by Cissy Wechter
and David Wechter

PRICE STERN SLOAN
Los Angeles

TO BARBARA, who fortunately was not an inspiration for this book.

DW

TO JULIUS, without whom I wouldn't have a co-author.

CW

Illustrations by Rick Penn-Kraus

Copyright © 1987 by Cissy Wechter and David Wechter
Illustrations copyright © 1987 by Price Stern Sloan, Inc.
Published by Price Stern Sloan, Inc.
360 North La Cienega Boulevard, Los Angeles, California 90048

ISBN: 0-8431-4704-0

WHAT THE WHINE EXPERTS ARE SAYING ABOUT THIS BOOK

"There aren't enough *pictures.*"

"It's too *expensive.*"

"Do I *have* to read this book?"

INTRODUCTION

Like laughing and crying, whining is an instinctive human trait. At about the same time we learn to speak, we learn to whine. But although we begin Whinemaking in early childhood . . .

. . . the process is nurtured during adolescence . . .

. . . and only fully developed during adulthood.

Whine connoisseurs point out that whinemaking has been around since the dawn of humankind. Examples from American history alone date back to such vintage whines as Paul Revere's infamous, "I just put the horse in the *stable*!" But every great culture is distinguished by its whines. Our world heritage is rich with classic whines from the past such as these:

Napoleon: My *hand* is cold!

Lincoln: We went to the theatre *last* night!

Henry VIII: Divorce lawyers are too *expensive*!

Betsy Ross: I'm *out* of green thread. I only have red, white, and *blue*!

Jesus: Dad, I don't *want* to go into the family business!

Alexander Graham Bell: If that's for me, tell them I'm not *home*!

King Arthur: I wanted a *square* table!

Moses: These tablets are too *heavy*!

It is with the goal of furthering the art of Whine Appreciation that this book is written.

The first section of this book contains important guidelines on the practice of whining and should be read thoroughly.*

You too, can learn to be a Whinemaster. Just follow these simple guidelines:

1. Learn to speak with a nasal voice.

2. Speak slowly. Drag your sentences out for as long as possible.

3. Emphasize the Key Word in your whine. Note how this helps convey your agony:

   "But you *promised* we could stop at Tiffany's!"

4. Stretch your Key Word so that it lasts for several seconds. Beginners may find it helpful to use longer words. For example:

   Try whining the word: "*Mom!*"
   Now, whine the word: "*Mother!*"

   Do you see how much more miserable and irritating the two-syllable version sounds? Eventually, you will learn how to stretch out even the shortest words:

   "I don't wanna *go-o-o-o-o-o!*"

5. Be sure you correctly determine *which* word to emphasize. See how the meaning of the following whine changes, depending on which word is stressed:

   "*We* never get to go to Europe!"

---

*Note: If your immediate reaction to that sentence was to complain out loud, "I don't *wanna* read all this stuff," then you are already a skilled whiner. You may skip these pages and go on to the rest of the book.

"We *never* get to go to Europe!"
"We never get to go to *Europe*!"

6. True Whine Experts are never satisfied—even after they've got what they've been whining for. If you've been whimpering all day to be taken to the zoo, don't stop once you get there. Find more things to whine about:

   "It's *dirty* here! It *smells* funny! It's too *hot*! When can we go *home*?"

7. Whenever possible, compare yourself to everyone else in the world:

   "Everybody gets to have their wedding at the Plaza except *me*!"

We could go on about timing, diction, grammar, *etc.*, but we're *tired* of explaining this. It's too *hard*! Haven't you got the *idea* yet?!

Now that you've learned about key words, for each whine below, determine the proper word to best express your anguish. The first example has been completed for you.

Can I have a *party*?

It's hot outside.

Do we have to have a babysitter?

We never get to have pizza.

When can I get a two-wheeler?

Mary's mother lets her stay up late.

Can we go skiing?

My shoelace is untied.

My purse is too heavy.

FAMOUS WHINEMASTERS

John McEnroe

Rodney Dangerfield

Johnny Ray

Lucy Ricardo

Tommy Smothers

Jim and
Tammy Faye Bakker

Ferdinand and
Imelda Marcos

Jerry Lewis

Portnoy

Garry Shandling

Eric Dickerson

Truman Capote

Richard Nixon

Richard Simmons

Rex Reed

Barney Fife, Aunt Bea,
Opie, Floyd and
Howard Sprague

Laverne and Shirley

Lisa Lubner

SELECTING THE RIGHT WHINE

Knowing how to choose the proper whine is an acquired skill in the whinemaker's art. The following exercise was designed to help you develop your technique. Fill in the blanks by choosing the appropriate whines from each column.

WHINES FOR ANY OCCASION

"I'm so sick of __A__! My __B__ is killing me! I feel like __C__. Could you __D__ for me?"

A	B	C	D
work	boss	crying	make an excuse
school	head	quitting	do my homework
the kids	migraine	a slave	drive the carpool
shopping	stomach	barfing	go to the drug store
sex	back	an animal	start divorce proceedings

WHINES FOR MEDICINAL PURPOSES

"Doctor, I'm having trouble with __A__. It hurts when I __B__. Could you reduce __C__? I want __D__."

A	B
my weight	move
your diagnosis	hyperventilate
my sex life	touch my you-know-what
depression	slash my wrists

C	D
my hips	a husband
your bill	a second opinion
my libido	your receptionist
my anxieties	a refill on my sleeping pills

TABLE WHINES

I want the *big* piece.

Liver's *gross*.

Can I be *excused*?

I *ate* too much.

DRY WHINES

I'm *thirsty*!

Can I just get my *feet* wet?

I need the *humidifier.*

It's *your* turn to water the plants.

My *lips* are always chapped.

Do I *have* to wait an hour to go swimming?

Can we go to *Disneyland*?

Can we get a *tennis court*?

Can we get a *swimming pool*?

It's *smoggy* outside.

Do we have *earthquake* insurance?

Whine, Women and Song

Joni Mitchell	Connie Francis
Joan Baez	Janice Ian
Phoebe Snow	Lesley Gore

* * * * * * * * * * * *

"It's My Party And I'll Cry If I Want To"

"Daddy Took The T-Bird Away"

"I Can't Get No Satisfaction"

"Let Me Be The One"

"It's Been A Hard Day's Night"

"Don't Make Me Wait For You"

"You Made Me Love You"

"Don't You Want Me?"

"Raindrops Keep Falling On My Head"

"You Don't Bring Me Flowers Anymore"

"I Cried For You"

ITALIAN WHINES

My Maserati gets only four kilometers to the *liter*!

Can we go to *Gucci*?

Do I have to learn *accordion*?

KOSHER WHINES

Do I have to go to *Hebrew* school?

Can I read the *New* Testament?

All the other kids get sandwiches on *white* bread.

Why can't *we* get a Christmas tree?

Are we having *deli* again?

My *yarmulke* keeps falling off.

It's *hard* to read from right to left.

My *parachute* won't open.

Do I have to pay tax on my *lottery* winnings?

How much longer do we have to stay in this *bomb* shelter?

Why does there have to be an eclipse just when I want to get a *suntan*?

How much longer are you going to be on the *phone*?

Would somebody help me fold these *sheets*?

I just waxed the *floor.*

Who put celery down the *garbage* disposal?

Could you bring me some *toilet* paper?

Could you ask your mother to stay in her *room*?

Whining and Dining

Could you bring the dressing on the *side*?

Is this *de*-caf?

I ordered my pasta al *dente*.

Could we sit by the *window*?

We wanted a *booth*.

Don't you have anything in *non*-smoking?

Could you leave out the *MSG*?

Light Whines

Is this *scale* right?

Is *brown* rice a starch?

Does lettuce *count*?

I *hate* diet dressing.

May I subtract a pound for my *socks*?

BLUSH WHINES

Do I *have* to undress for P.E.?

I think my *deodorant* just stopped working.

Does this stain *show*?

Do I have to give an *oral* report?

Is there something stuck in my *teeth*?

RED WHINES

Why can't I read "*Lolita*"?

Do I have to wear a *babushka*?

Can we go to *West* Berlin?

Do I have to finish my *borscht*?

HOUSE WHINES

Can we get a *maid*?

Do I have to take out the *garbage*?

Can we let the *dog* in?

Can we eat *out*?

Can we *redecorate*?

How come you never lost weight when we were *married*?

I want the car *and* the house!

Your check's *late* again.

My Photo Album

There were
too many
__bees__!

Everybody
else looks
great.

We broke __up__
the next day.

I hate
my __hair__.

DAYS OF WHINE AND ROSES

It's too *hot* to mow the lawn.
All the flowers are *dead*.
Could we just plant *ivy*?
Can we get a *gardener*?
There are *bugs* out there.

SACRAMENTAL WHINES

Do I have to go to *confession*?
When will Lent be *over*?
I said grace *last* night.
Everybody *else* gets to commit sins.

JAPANESE WHINES

I'm *sick* of rice.

I tore my *kimono*.

My *saki's* cold.

Will you tie my *obi*?

Why didn't *we* win the war?

There's no *future* in being a Kamakazi.

I don't *want* to commit Hari Kari.

RHINE WHINES

Do we have to listen to *Wagner*?

Bratwurst gives me *gas*.

Do I have to read *Hesse*?

Why didn't *we* win the war?

FRENCH WHINES

Could we go to the *Riviera*?

There's nothing *good* playing at Cannes.

I don't *understand* Sartre.

Could we live on the *Left* Bank?

Nothing at Dior looked *good* on me.

GIFTS FOR WHINERS

It doesn't matter what you give them, because they are going to return it anyway.

Was it good for *you*?

I have a *headache*.

You're *never* in the mood.

Are you *sure* the kids are asleep?

That's too *kinky*!

I don't *like* whipped cream.

Waterbeds make me *seasick*.

We already *tried* that position.

You're blocking the *video*.

HALF LITERS

Can we get a *dog*?

Do I have to wear my headgear to *school*?

I want my *own* room.

I *never* get to stay up late.

When can *I* get a bra?

Do I have to *practice*?

What did you *bring* me?

Can I ride in *front*?

Can I sit by the *window*?

Can I have a *slumber* party?

I have to go to the *bathroom.*

Dear Mom and Dad,

    I <u>hate</u> camp. It's <u>boring</u>. I miss my <u>TV</u> shows. They make us play <u>outdoors</u>. I'm <u>homesick</u>. The kids here don't <u>like</u> me. Come <u>get</u> me.

        Your son,

           Stanley

P.S. I didn't <u>want</u> to write a letter. They <u>made</u> me.

SPARKLING WHINES

I wanted a *four* carat diamond.

I can't get my *ring* off.

I wanted *opera* length pearls.

These earrings are too *heavy*.

WHITE WHINES

Don't you have *American* cheese?

Where did you put my Lawrence *Welk* records?

Is this neighborhood *safe*?

Aged Whines

You never *visit* me anymore.

I don't *need* a hearing aid. *What?*

I can't find my *glasses.*

I'VE GOT ONE TOOTH *LEFT* IN MY MOUTH, AND IT <u>ACHES</u>.

Expensive Whines

It's *hard* to park a Cadillac.

Would you speak to the *help*?

The masseuse is *late* again.

I forgot to wind my *Rolex.*

Why don't *you* gas up the Rolls?

THE AGING PROCESS

A fine whine is timeless. As it ages, its character will mature, but its essence will remain the same.

Aged 5 years
I want a *bicycle*.

I *hate* girls.

I don't *want* to get a haircut.

The tooth fairy only left me a *quarter.*

17 years
I want a *motorcycle*.

I don't have a date for the *prom*.

What's *wrong* with purple hair?

When do I get my *braces* off?

40 years

I want a *new* car.

I don't *want* to see a marriage counselor.

Do you notice any *grey*?

My gums are *bleeding*.

70 plus years

I want a *motorized* wheelchair.

Stop looking at other women in the *therapy* pool.

Is my *toupee* on straight?

I can't find my *dentures*.

IMPORTED WHINES

I can't get parts for my *Saab*.

These instructions are in *Japanese*.

No one in my English class speaks *English*.

I don't *want* to try sushi.

My *kilt* itches.

Do I *have* to join Little League?

But I *like* the library.

Do we *have* to get a dog?

ABOUT THE AUTHORS

CISSY WECHTER

When I'm not writing, I spend my time at Flair, my boutique in Encino, the Whine Capitol of California. But I live in *Studio City,* and it's so far to *drive.* I have two wonderful sons and a grandson, Max, but he moved to *Denver* and I hardly ever *see* him! I wrote the lyrics to my husband's hit song, "Spanish Flea," which was recorded over eighty times, but most of the records were *instrumental.*

DAVID WECHTER

My *real* profession is writing and directing motion pictures like *Midnight Madness* and *The Malibu Bikini Shop.* I didn't want to co-write this book, but my mother *made* me! I wanted *my* name to be first, but she said it had to be *alphabetical.*

OTHER BOOKS BY THE AUTHORS
"Whinesburg, Ohio"
"Whiney the Pooh"
"*Sour* Grapes of Wrath"
"*Whining* at Bridge"